A person who will always help you try to find the answer. A man who never gives in, always there to listen and to discuss his views. A shoulder to lean on and a hand to help. A truthful person who knows what to say and when. But he also knows when to say nothing.

To my mother, Marie Rugg, my father, Freddie Rugg, and my sister, Jane Rugg, much gratitude and respect for your nursing and caring given to me with tremendous love.

To my great uncle, Philip Magnus, my uncle, David Polden, and friend, David Marks. You all showed me great love and patience, helped me within my life in eventually reaching the recovery line. Thank you; for without you six people, my words within this book would never be read.

Philip Rugg

LOOKING FOR THE KEY

AUSTIN MACAULEY PUBLISHERS™
LONDON • CAMBRIDGE • NEW YORK • SHARJAH

A CIP catalogue record for this title is available from the British Library.

ISBN 9781528994149 (Paperback)
ISBN 9781528994156 (ePub e-book)

www.austinmacauley.com

First Published (2020)
Austin Macauley Publishers Ltd
25 Canada Square
Canary Wharf
London
E14 5LQ

The nurses and doctors at Oldchurch Hospital, Romford. Also the doctors and staff at Forest Edge Practice, Hainault. You are the reason why I am still here. Thank you.

All Washed Up

I need my space, I am sorry for it to end this way
I will not let it be a drawn-out affair, it must end today
Time has now passed and all my love and trust has gone
I know that you keep on saying sorry, but what you do is wrong
Having tried to contain my feeling, about my resentment towards you
The vows that we took a long, long time ago have been broken, and my regret
is saying I do
You keep on saying sorry, just give me another chance
And the feelings of pity I portray to you, by always holding out the olive
branch
No more, no more, I say but it always ends the same
As ever a tear appears on your cheek as the tides are once more turned and I
take the blame
I just won't go on holding the towel and cleaning up after your lies
I always have to start again, so we must just stop and say our goodbyes
So let us put our time together behind us and just please let me go
For the pain we share together will be all that is left to show
You just try to understand why I must break from this rag within our sink
Just let me go, become free, and break your holding link
So I cannot forgive and will not be forced into cleaning another cup
I will never quite understand why you must always wash and I have to dry up.

Calmness of the View

The scene that I see, the look of beauty quite serene
I lay on top of the hill, longing to be at forever, never to be seen
I long for, pray for the vision never to end
The overhanging branches of the silver birch, moss field earth and the river that
bends
To see it is truly unreal, the windward clouds, afar, falling away over the
faraway mill
The sun reflecting on the valley below, as if it were yet to be still
It helps me with my thoughts to write and compose
As this is the only true aspect which I have chose'
And the expanse of green evolving before me, trying to take over my feelings
The richness of breeze around always forever, holding, smiling and healing
I just wish that you, my love, could be here for me to feed my hunger
But I will wait, for one day you will be with me to share this wonder.

Could It Be Me

Is it you that I see, or would you say me
For it's you that I would most want to try and be
By my left as always, awaiting right by the port side
Showing that you still have love for me, of some kind
They hope to see that we will finally be as one
With no other troubles, clouding over our shadow-hidden sun
I long for your heart to come back, as referred to myself
That will be only you, my dear, sharing my love and near wealth
And so I will just have to wait, for your love to come back true
From other people that you lost and discarded, just as I have lost you.

Could You

If I could, can you could I
If you would, can you could I
If I need you, can you could I
If I love you to, can you could I
If I can't, can you could I
If I do see you, can you could I
When I try to say to you I could
I can't can you, goodbye.

Difference

There are some people who are not quite alike
People bully them and look for a fight
Tease and bedazzle, laugh and giggle
They say, "Why are you not like me, as fit as a fiddle?"
But these people who they jest and taunt
Are head and shoulders above you and their thoughts
They look upon life, with eyes wide open and blue
No frowns or long faces, like others and you
They laugh and smile, and enjoy life, that's true
I just ask, what have these so brave beings ever done to you?

Filling My Shoes

You try so hard to quietly step inside
For your frustration in not achieving, you just cannot hide
Our outlooks on life have become so diverse, you never will
Twist your instep, curl your toes, just not meant to be, they are just too big to fill
You must just admit that you show no mercy or heart
I show my open hand to others, but all you do is just part
We both understand that I myself don't want my shoes for you to slip into
Just look elsewhere, for we both know that 'filling my shoes' you are just not meant to.

Flowering unto Me

When I look and find in my mind the scene of you
Roses abundant and the aromatic fragrance between us two
The fresh green lawn and flowers that blossom
For it is just you that I long to bear, by your tempting me from top to bottom
The aroma we reach holds no untold bounds
Like the steady oak tip tree above the moss field ground
And I swear that my love for you holds me in constant fear
As I hold onto you, never to release, trying and be near
You being so true is all that can be held by myself to and some
For together as in union, always your shoulder I lean to, always there for me to
overcome.

For Me to Be

I think a lot about what to beat and the best way to decide
And I work out the result before I can run and hide
I just wish to know what is best for me
For people to want and for you to just look and see
I have myself and my views to listen, sometimes I find the key
But alone I feel, even if someone is there, hoping that they just long to be
I fret and frown most days, still not at ease
Having no one around whom I would try to please
But I am stuck within this shut tightly hell
Waiting for someone to appear and help me crack this clasping shell.

For Others to Know

The light that I had before
The light that no other, only you saw
We are lovers who are secretly as one
As we don't allow everyone to see, only some
You are the only lady that truly holds my thoughts
When I see your palmed open hand, just for my heart to be caught
I long for the steel door to be opened, to release us from this rock
So we must seek and find the key together, and turn it to unlock
Our being together will damage others who really should have no say
But as we both know as told. These forces will hold our love at bay
Be patient, my partner, and soon I will be able to pronounce my feelings for
you
For others to see, and ourselves to show, our love to all, and not only the few.

KO of Homeboy

This really should be a fight to savour
In which the two pugilists will be doing each other no favour
The public have been waiting for this bout a while and some
Let's hope our boy defends the title, which he has won
The bell goes, 'Round 1' gets underway, as the home lad hunts his fearful prey
Left, right he jabs, the other guy holds him, bows down, then pushes the champ
away
Upper cut, right hook, then a left, they all catch
As the crowd go wild, at the start of what they hope will become a sided match
For the audience, well, by now know that the challenger is ready to diminish
Another right and left by our man, looks like near to a finish
But hold on, no, no, the rival has just caught our man cold
Another combination, as our boy begins to fold
The crowd gasps as a left puts their hero to the ropes
It's looking like our man just cannot defend himself and cope
I cannot believe what I am about to tell
Their one-time boxing idol, knocked out cold as he fell Everyone is stunned as
he lays directly on his back, we are all praying that he beats the count
And the ref carries on with his reciting the numbers, "9, 10, you are out!"
Well, listeners, the upset has just not been to order
As the new pugilist king holds his arms aloft with the help of his jubilant
corner.

I Have No Memory

"I have no memory, for what you have said that I have done
For I assure you, kind sir, it was not me, this theft could have been by almost anyone
I have never taken or stolen what is not rightfully mine
So I will thank you, Officer, to look elsewhere and find another suspect to sign
To be wrongfully accused hurts, by your unfair and forceful claims
It just seems to me, Constable, that you are just looking for someone to blame
So, sir, if you have no charges forthcoming, I will be on my way
I thank you, Inspector, and I wish you well, and that you all have a nice day."
Will they never learn, I smile as I walk with my left hand in my trouser pocket
Caressing the ladies' purse which I have just obtained, along with her beautiful golden locket
She should have been more careful by keeping her satchel closed
For then no one like me could lift her belongings and have it on in their toes.

If Not You

Is it you which I see or is it me
I cannot think how this will settle and be
Either a look or glance from you I need
For which I know what you can't do, just forgive my greed
All I miss is to just hear you breathe
A sigh or word, in which I will try to thieve
Forgive me, my dear for my tease and jaunts
As I will try to hold my damning thoughts
For I know that we can never be one
The moon now will always be there instead of the setting sun
If it is not just you, who will be mine to keep
Now that you are gone, it is time for us both to sleep.

Our Musical Minds Collide

Our thoughts collide when we discuss the plot
We sometimes disagree with the ideas that we have suddenly got
But our roles within the verse, we both know are needed
As the words and sounds that we write and compose are taken and heeded
We sit and narrate until the near, clear conclusion
As turns are made, one listens, the other talks, as if a literary transfusion
Without your influence, my words could never quite come across
And the world of composing by lyrics and tune would be at a very serious loss.

Knowledge

London is the capital of the world
As I put its places and streets in my mind, which are hard to be held
Driving along every day on my bike
Looking around at whatever I like
The cold mornings aren't so bad
But it's the pouring rain that drives you mad
The black cab drivers look at me with regret
Knowing they were here too, which they want to just forget
Balls to it all, I say each evening
Why should I do it, what am I learning
Dole money, that's a joke
You can give it to another bloke
Well, it's goodbye for now, I say that with very much disdain
For I'm getting out of this knowledge lark, it's driving me bloody insane.

Let Me See

Let me see if tonight will be
Together at last, just yourself and me
I pine for your touch and typical laughter
And crave for your attention, for now and the hereafter
My thoughts are with you within our closed shell
Always wanting to pick you up and embrace after you fell
But we had better save our wishing love for another day
For today, if it is not right, it's just for us, and not those others to say
So if we cannot help ourselves to love and become
We will ask our lord for help to emerge as one
We must try and remedy the problem to be solved
By us both talking and listening, and to be told
I desire you more and do not want anything as much
And I know that if it is returned, it will be you that I long for and touch.

Listen and See

Listen and see, for I want to tell you again
Look at me. Christ, you're driving me insane
Come over here, no, not over there
Stop acting like you don't really care
Just think about things too and heed my advice
Stop trying to be so damned bloody nice
Be yourself and don't get misled
For time's a great healer, or so it's said
If you enjoy life, hear me again
Just try and think of others who you show no pain
Step back, for no harm is never truly meant
Find out from others it is not sent by vicious lies or intent.

My Cup Half Full

The time that I take to think things through
About the thoughts and longing that I have always held towards you
And as I sit and try to work out just why
My hand approaches your heart, to touch, just for you to say goodbye
Why have you done this, for I don't understand
For helping you fall out of love spurn my open-palmed hand
I have always succeeded in giving you your wishes, everything that you desire
And all that you show me in return is rebuff and no warmth or fire
If only you could return my love, however meagre or small
And fill up my empty glass, for it has now become only half full.

My Love Not Returned

All that I have in this short time is you
My being is always wanting to be the centre of your truth
Your comebacks to my feelings are not well meant
I want my desire for you returned to some extent
But you never clutch hold of the back of my outward hand
As if there is no love from you to me there to be found
For if it is not returned, I will eventually find another
And it will be for you, my love, to lose, as you will find no other.

My Open Flower You

As your light falls down upon unto me
My smile opens up for you and each to see
You are my eternal rose bud, ready to flower and bloom
If as a rush of pollen, a beautiful fragrance, as only you enter the room
When your aromatic aroma arrives, pure and fresh as a newly budding seedling
The scent that you hold emits feelings and guidance – it shows me the way just
by your leading
I believe others succumb for me to love, but for you it is never undone, making
me glad that I am your son
For I know that you will always be there as my mother, helping me beat it and
finally overcome
As you come alive in the spring, as a youth in her teenage time
And flourish within the summer months, inspiring me to compose this rhyme
As the autumn arrives, others like myself begin to wilt and fade away
But we look up onto you to stay solid, open, still there, just as you are today
Winter arrives but the garden is bare, with just yourself and our Robin Freddie
to see
So I thank you, my lord, for her light to shine through, no, not for all, just for
me.

No Left Jab

As a young man, I was told I was destined to become
A pugilist, which my grandfather was one
I longed for this dream to develop and evolve
But for my poor left hand, which I found hard to solve
By hitting the punchbag draped from the ceiling
Then jabbing at my father's hand as he would be kneeling
For I admire the craft of two men in the ring
They do not know each other on the outside, as they soon would within
They fight in union as combat, the winner I cannot always tell
Until the victor stands up, arms held aloft at the final bell
I respect these men where fear holds no thought
A trait that you are born with and that can never be bought.

Not Me

If I look upon your head held high
I just see your eyes and I ask myself why
Being with you is so hard to bear
For I know truly that you really don't care
My feelings for yourself are just not returned
For your hand I wanted, with which you spurned
So I will go and leave your side and let the time pass by
Now that I know that you could only mean to say just goodbye.

Now and Then

If I could fly, I'd soar in the sky
Up in the heavens, just saying goodbye
I care for nothing when I fly
To my troubles that I once knew that made me cry
I ponder over my thoughts that I had down below
Just hoping that they will finally give up and let go
But now that I know that some things are always here to stay
Except myself, for I hope to fly along long way some day.

Out of the Game

A saying of mine I use quite a lot
The line about me and something I got
To me it comes across as truly a fact
These special four words I use but with tact
I have a lot of memories, mostly sad and blue
When I did not know really what to do
I used the saying off hand and glib
But for those long years ago, it was no fib
Thinking about it, I thought off the pain
And at long last now, I've finally
CAME BACK INTO THE GAME.

About You

When I see you, I weep and sigh
And I look at you and I ask myself why
You should try and forget, smile, and it will come true
To a beautiful waif of a girl just like you
Your heart is a thing that cannot be bought
And with charm and soul that you give out with very much thought
You should be pleased you have found out who you really are
And you will reach that loved one's heart without travelling too far.

Your Number's Up

If I knew we would be 1
We would see us 2, so much more than some
I'd always release you and set you 3
4 I know you will always come back to me
5, 6, 7 times you always return to see
For I'd 8 to be left alone, if it is not meant to be
9 for a word I never use with you, for it means if not so
I will see you at 10, and then we can go.

The Jockeys to Blame

As I open the paper, knowing what's to come
I head straight for the pages where the horses will run
I always promise myself not to gamble away my so-called bread and butter
But the addiction's too great for myself to have another flutter
As I walk to the vein of my life, hoping and believing
That my luck will change, and it will be me who is thieving
I lay money on the first, my horse comes second by a head
It was the jockey's fault I state, for he should have led
The next three races go as the one before
Lost, beaten, unlucky, as I edge to the door
One last wager as I divert to study the form
And here's a winner I can see, the tipsters forecast it warm
I place my last ten pounds, praying for it to win
But the rider pushed too late, another jockey sin?
So I trudge to the outlet, pockets are bare
No money for even a bus ride, for I can't afford the fare
So I must look on the bright side, as I say to myself
As there is always another day to try and reclaim my wealth.

The Solver Switch

Brr, brr, brr, the chudder of the deep chucks
Against the butt of the drill heads, they weave and tuck
Whilst making me shudder with frightening terror
As they grind nonstop endlessly together
Whenever I hear this rotation of a screaming noise
My eyes split apart, seemingly ready and poised
To look into each gaping wound within my purple gums
My fists grip the rails, waiting for my hurting vocal shrieks to become numb
Please someone cut the cable. The noise is turning me completely unstable
Could someone help me turn off this ghostly malarkey?
Thank you, at last the mains are cut and his flexible arm no more sparky
Please be gone, go away fast
Until the next alarm, my lord, let this time last.

Wait for Me

For it is you that I long for and love
Who has departed this earth to go up above
My head becomes content when I begin to feel your thoughts
Holding on to our time together that we had, which just can never be bought
I hold these ideas close, for no one can see
Gripping, clasping, never to let go, so to become free
To recall thy love within on my palmed open hand
Never forgotten or tried to be hidden within our beach-topped sand
I long to see your smile when I join you once again and finally go
And rekindle our love for us both to be as one and once more to show.

Wide Open

The space I see so open to view
A scene I know just for us two
The swaying trees with their buds opening around
A delicious sight from the moss field ground
As the roses bloom, not caring who sees
Their fragrance arises in the calming breeze
I want this beautiful view never to end
This scene should be wrapped for myself to send
I know it will not last just until our God wants it to go
For the moment, my lord, I thank you for just my show.

Yesteryear

The songs and acts of yesteryear
With performances of a kind we hold so dear
Dancers, singers and their acting too
Giving their best to show for me and you
Jolsen the master who could do all three
His songs live forever, 'Mammi', 'California' and 'Climb upon My Knee'
Then there was Jimmy Cagney, the man called to play the tough guy
But could he dance, rhyme, tap. God, he could fly
Jimmy Stewart, the actor no one came near
Spectacular in the film 'What a Wonderful Life', which always brings a tear
Chaplin, the king of silence, who made you believe
That in his films the underdog can always achieve
Lady Thespians, who was there also, to be admired about
Dietrich, Mansfield, Hepburn and that Monroe pout
I have not forgot Brando the actor we all loved to see
Mostly his portrayal in the 'Godfather' films as Don Corleone
Just a few greats of the golden age that we admire on their show
Who will never be forgotten by us, so just try not to let go.

You Never Saw Me

If you could look, the sight would be me
What would you try and want to see
For it is not your right to want some other
To view and look down on to me just like my mother
To help you find what you seek and recover
So just stop looking for me, as you might never discover
That I am a person that takes you as I have known
Selfish, complicated, you have never once grown
Listen not to other thoughts, showing them no care, just your way
Never letting myself have time for, with opinion or right to say
We will never become one, we are too far apart
So you must think of the past we once journeyed, not the start
Goodbye, my once love, memories I hold are so true
My love has flown to another, so sad that it has not landed at you.

Your Way

When I see you look at certain things
Your eyes come alive and fly, as if they have wings
Your cheeks become a musty red that soon comes alight
And your smile appears so true to me by sight
I have thoughts that I portray about you, that I cannot let go
For me always to hold, and for you just to show
I keep my strong feelings about my desire for you that runs too deep
And I hope that in your company, I will open up for only you to keep
I show my love for you in this writing, please try and give it some meaning
To a lass that I betroth my heart, my love and my feelings.

Blaky Boy's Team Talk

Blaky Boy gave us his usual motivating team talk today
If we win this game, we can go all the way
Keep your shape we will play our usual four, four, two,
Kypo, always take on the left back, make 'em scared of you
Older Roasty Dal, you stay up front, and keep doing what you do
Scoring goals, volleys, side footers, even back heelers too.
Davey boy you keep the back four steady, giving them their roles
Telling Geofrro and Nicky, get crosses in for your brother Dal to score his goals
In midfield I want Harris to take on players, giving and going with the ball
Letting Toddy play a bit deeper, and Bobby boy listen to his calls
Marksy and the Harding brothers play together as a unit, cos you three are one
The best trio ever, bar only some,
Lastly, our Goalie Webby, try and dive around a bit, don't listen to the crowd
who keep singing, "Come on Webby, catch it."
I think our team talk is over, let's just play football nice and stable
STUART YOU STOPPED PLAYING WITH YOUR SUBBUTTEO YET, FOR
YOUR DINNER IS ON THE TABLE.

My Uncle Phil Is a Gift

Your company for me to be in, is a time when I am most at rest,
To hear your voice, cackle with laughter, in comical jest,
With your hands being thrown describing us your thoughts and actions of this
day
Over indulgent, elaborate, even demeaning, well only some would say,
But the untold joy that you emit from the stories that you tell,
Brings a smile to everyone that you know so well,
Your comic verse and charm are for all to see and cherish
Without these words that you share so lovingly and true, helping our bad
thoughts and feelings to fly away and perish.
Joy to be in your company, the key to your words, is there to be found
For everyday your company is a gift within, thank you, for showing me your
hand.

For Others to Know

The light that I had before
The light that no other, only you saw
We are lovers who are secretly as one
As we don't allow everyone to see, only some
You are the only lady that truly holds my thoughts
When I see your palmed open hand, for only my heart there to be caught
I long for the steel door to be opened, to release us from this rock
So we must seek and find the key together, and turn it to unlock
Our being together will damage others, who really should have no say
But as we both know, as told, these forces will try and hold our love at bay
Be patient my partner and soon I will be able to pronounce my feelings for you
For ourselves to show, so others can see, that our love for each other is the
utmost to me.

Give Me Peace of Mind

Just answer my question, be truthful and fair
Stop acting like you have no feelings for me and don't really care
But if those are your thoughts, explain to me and put me at ease
By telling me what you want in your life, and how I can please
If you let me go it will be your loss of the greatest love I give
Your silence on the matter of us, is filled with holes which are open and will
drip through the sieve
Just show your feelings, tell what I can do
And give me the peace of mind as I always give back to you.

I Do

As I turn, just wanting you to see
A scene of beauty, walking towards me
With people we love and care all attending
All with us to view our words that we will both be sending
In God our father's house, we share this moment together
As I hold out my hand, which you embrace for now and forever
You turn to look at, what you have seen before
The love in our eyes firmly sealed, both at peace again, once more
The minister asks us questions, as to why we must be true to one another
Making me hold your hand more tightly, as for me here will be no other
I wait for the reply to my unanswered question that I have just asked you
As you look at me with your beautiful eyes and simply say
I DO

It's Not Your Time to Go

As my eyes were closed, to those people who cared
I just lay there hoping, and longing for my life to be spared
With my thoughts still there, at what still I had not done
My mind turned to anger, what a waste I had become
In your arriving at my side, my hopes, still waiting to be shared,
You, smiling at me grandfather, and asking, wake up my son, arise from your
sleep, you still have so much to be heard.
As you who had gone a long time, before
Touching my brow as I kissed your hand again, once more.
You sigh as you speak, the voice that had never left my thoughts
It is not your time to go boy, boy, it's not your time, for now to be caught.
Relief appeared to me, as my grandfather said words, I had longed to hear
Stay aware and your pain will soon be gone, no longer for you to suffer and
bear
Do not leave from here yet, only when it is your time, then you can come
But not yet, for as you know, you have still not completed, you are not yet done
My Grandpa's, hand, left my head as his smiling face began to recede
As my eyes open directly to loved ones, making me thankful, to hear and to see
As I looked around wanting to see my mother's father, once more
But he had gone, for his work was done, with me, he had reopened my life's
front door.

Knowing You

No one knows you as I do
Some people try, but can never get through
With time we can laugh, smile, share a thought or even cry
As you can find my shoulder to lean, and I won't ask why
People try to understand that our feelings and thoughts are combined
To others who look and hunt for a love like ours which is hard to find
I desire you as I believe it is returned to me, as well
For no one to see or hear and only for us to tell.

Nothing to Show

You were always just a trinket on my arm
For me to show to others, and for you to charm
All we had was fantasy, a dream not real
As romance, love and affection, as time stood still
I regret that you have no passion towards me to give
My showing off you to others, is for what I live
You treated me as a bit part player, who you beckoned to come near to
And showing no sense or reason, as you have no love for me to share
I do not succeed in breaking free from your strangle hold
As you look at me with pity, you speak no more, not being told
I now know my love that you are the charm that I wanted myself to display
As away my love must go, never to return to you as of today.

One of a Kind

You are a backbone to many
And a shoulder for everyone and not just for me
A lady who when needed will find the answer for each and everyone to see
The mould was broken after you came into being
For there is only one girl who brings me guidance with her love and leading
A sister I could never do without, you being a special part of my life
Helping me to find the answer and solve my old strife
Now it's your turn to be given and receive the love that you always emit
So I thank you my dear sister for being the candle for me, as always fully lit.

Runs Deep

Your blood runs deep
Threw my gaping open hands
Your feelings are just like mine
For that I don't understand
My need is just for your shoulder to be besides and lean
Within this time, I believe you a dear friend, as you have always been
To me that is all I can wish for, being with you and no other,
Love from me always coming from you Dear Younger Brother.

Voice of Its Own

I write things down, which I find comes at a flow
Verse, lyric and storey, as my imagination seems to grow
I do not try to think too deep, about outcome, love or why
But with a simple ease it arrives, with me not having to try
Me taking the credit, for the creation of this written, scripted art
As contentment reaches my thoughts, as no one else but me has played a part
No I am blind, for there is a blade that has helped me look into the deep
unknown
For it is only the pen, which can deliver a voice, free from my help
And just on its own.

Why Should I Write

What I ask is the reason that I compose
For will anyone learn, from what I have told
I give words to my thoughts that I find and see
Concerning my loves, feelings which mean something to me
To people who read my lyrics and take some guidance
For no one can confirm this all that I hear is silence
But I will continue to try to get someone to note my poems somewhat
As it will be the people's loss if I am not noted, and just seemingly forgot.